NATIONAL GEOGRAPHIC

The Nez Perce

People of the Northwest

A HISTORICAL LOOK AT NATIVE AMERICANS

Ruby Maile

PICTURE CREDITS
Cover: © Christie's Images/Corbis/Tranz

page 1 © Corbis/Tranz; page 4 (left); Photodisc; page 4 (right), Corbis; page 5 (top) © Dave G. Houser/Corbis/Tranz; page 5 (bottom), Photodisc; page 6 © David Muench/Corbis/Tranz; page 7, Digital Vision; page 8 (bottom), Photodisc; page 8 (top) © Ralph A. Clevenger/Corbis/Tranz; page 9, Photodisc; page 10 National Anthropological Archives, Smithsonian Institute, Neg 2923 A; page 11 © Photo courtesy of National Park Service, Nez Perce National Historical Park. Image number NEPE-HI-0686; page 14 (top) © Photo courtesy of National Park Service, Nez Perce National Historical Park. Image number NEPE 125-F; page 14 (bottom) © Dean Conger/Corbis/Tranz; page 15 © Werner Forman Archive; page 16 © MUSEUM OF THE ROCKIES/E.H.Latham/X77.25.77; page 18 © Photo courtesy of National Park Service, Nez Perce National Historical Park. Image number NEPE-8744; page 21 © Christie's Images/Corbis/Tranz; page 23 © Corbis/Tranz; page 24 © Christie's Images/Corbis/Tranz; page 25 © Photo courtesy of National Park Service, Nez Perce National Historical Park. Image number NEPE-HI-0824; page 26 © Jackson Sundown. ca. 1915. National Cowboy & Western Heritage Museum, Oklahoma City, OK; Outside back cover: (top left) © Christie's Images/Corbis/Tranz; (top right) © Horace Bristol/Corbis/Tranz; (bottom left) © Bettmann/Corbis/Tranz; (bottom right) © National Anthropological Archives, Smithsonian Institute, T.W. Smillie, Neg 73-9466.

Produced through the worldwide resources of the National Geographic Society, John M. Fahey, Jr., President and Chief Executive Officer; Gilbert M. Grosvenor, Chairman of the Board; Nina D. Hoffman, Executive Vice President and President, Books and Education Publishing Group.

PREPARED BY NATIONAL GEOGRAPHIC SCHOOL PUBLISHING
Ericka Markman, Senior Vice President and President, Children's Books and Education Publishing Group; Steve Mico, Vice President and Editorial Director; Marianne Hiland, Executive Editor; Richard Easby, Editorial Manager; Jim Hiscott, Design Manager; Kristin Hanneman, Illustrations Manager; Matt Wascavage, Manager of Publishing Services; Sean Philpotts, Production Manager.

EDITORIAL MANAGEMENT
Morrison BookWorks, LLC

PROGRAM CONSULTANTS
Dr. Shirley V. Dickson, Program Director, Literacy, Education Commission of the States; Margit E. McGuire, Ph.D., Professor of Teacher Education and Social Studies, Seattle University.

CONTENT REVIEWER
Willard Bill, Enrolled Member of the Muckleshoot Tribe, Auburn, Washington; College of Education, University of Washington.

National Geographic Theme Sets program developed by Macmillan Education Australia, Pty Limited.

Published by the National Geographic Society
1145 17th Street, N.W.
Washington, D.C. 20036-4688

ISBN: 978-0-7922-4726-5
ISBN: 0-7922-4726-4

Printed in China.

14 15 16 17 18 19 20 21
10 9 8 7 6

Contents

A Historical Look at Native Americans

Native Americans have lived in the United States for thousands of years, long before other peoples made their homes here. There are many different Native American nations or peoples, each with their own language, traditions, and way of life. These peoples include the Nez Perce, the Pueblos, the Iroquois, and the Cheyenne.

Key Concepts

1. **The homelands of native people have influenced their food, clothing, and shelter.**
2. **The stories and arts of native people were an expression of culture and a way of passing on values.**
3. **Early trade was a way of exchanging both goods and ideas.**

Native American Homelands of Long Ago

The Nez Perce

The Nez Perce lived along the rivers of the Northwest.

The Pueblos

The Pueblos lived in the Southwest.

This Nez Perce man is wearing traditional dress. In this book you will read about the history of the Nez Perce people.

The Iroquois

The Iroquois lived surrounded by the woods of the Northeast.

The Cheyenne

The Cheyenne lived on the flat grasslands of the central Plains.

The NEZ PERCE: People of the Northwest

The Nez Perce are a Native American group, or nation. They were called Nez Perce by French traders. The name means "pierced nose." But the Nez Perce did not pierce their noses. The traders mistook them for another group. The Nez Perce call themselves Nimi'ipu, which means "real people."

Key Concept 1 **The homelands of native people have influenced their food, clothing, and shelter.**

The Homeland of the Nez Perce

The homeland of the Nez Perce is in the Northwest. A group's homeland is usually the place where the group first lived. It can also be a place where the group moved to. Many Nez Perce still live in the Northwest today.

The Nez Perce homeland includes rivers and mountains.

homeland
the place a people or nation chooses to make its home

The Nez Perce homeland has swift rivers. The rivers follow valleys west to the Pacific Ocean. The homeland also has flat sections called Plains. The Plains are covered with grass. Animals such as bear, deer, and elk can be found there. The Nez Perce homeland also has many high mountains.

The Nez Perce hunted grizzly bears in the Northwest.

Location of Nez Perce Homeland

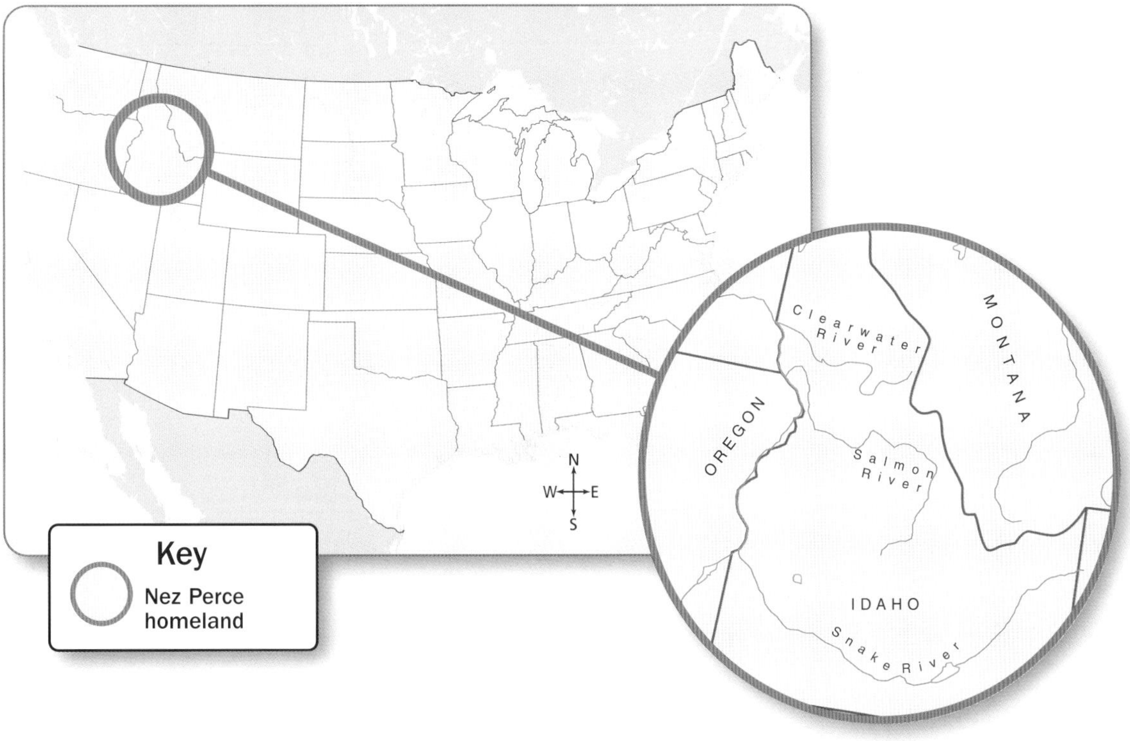

Food

The Nez Perce ate food that they found in their homeland. They moved with the changing seasons to hunt and gather food. One of their main foods was salmon from the rivers.

The Nez Perce fished for salmon in the spring.

During spring, a lot of salmon swim from the ocean up the rivers of the Northwest. The Nez Perce had their villages along these rivers. The men went to the rivers to fish. The women gathered nuts, roots, and berries. The salmon meat was dried and then stored for later.

By summer, there were fewer salmon coming into the rivers. The Nez Perce then moved to the mountains. There, they could hunt animals such as deer, elk, and mountain goats.

The Nez Perce hunted mountain goats in the summer.

Nez Perce Food Sources

Food Source	Spring	Summer	Fall	Winter
Fishing	✔		✔	
Hunting		✔	✔	✔
Gathering	✔	✔	✔	
Eating stored food				✔

In the fall, the weather in the mountains began to get cold. The Nez Perce returned to their villages by the rivers. The women went back to gathering roots such as camas root and bitterroot. The salmon returned to the rivers. The men went fishing again. They also continued hunting deer and elk.

Winter, too, was spent in their riverside villages. During the winter months, the Nez Perce lived on stored foods.

The Nez Perce hunted elk in the winter.

Clothing

The Nez Perce mostly wore clothes made from the skins of the animals they hunted. Both men and women wore **moccasins** on their feet. In winter, the moccasins were lined with fur to keep out the cold. People wore heavy deerskin and **bison** robes in winter to keep warm.

Men's Clothing

The Nez Perce men wore long, fringed shirts made of deerskin. They wore leggings and a type of short skirt called a **breechcloth**. Their clothes were decorated with elk's teeth, porcupine quills, shells, and beads. The women made these beads from shells and animal bone. Later, they got glass beads from European traders.

This Nez Perce man is wearing clothes decorated with beads and porcupine quills.

Women's Clothing

The Nez Perce women wore long, belted dresses made from deerskin. They used dyes to color their dresses. They made the dyes from vegetables or other materials that they found in their homeland. Their clothes were decorated with elk's teeth and porcupine quills. Sometimes they also used beads.

This Nez Perce woman is wearing a dress made from deerskin.

Shelter

The Nez Perce lived in several types of houses. In the summer, the Nez Perce needed houses that were easy to move from place to place. They needed houses that were easy to set up. **Tepees** were perfect for this. The Nez Perce covered the tepees with bison skins and tule mats. Tule is a plant that grew in the rivers in the Nez Perce homeland.

In the winter, the Nez Perce needed warm houses. They built large **longhouses** where several family groups could live. Longhouses were like a long series of tepees joined together.

Tule mats like these helped the Nez Perce of long ago keep rain out of tepees.

Key Concept 2 The stories and arts of native people were an expression of culture and a way of passing on values.

Language and Storytelling

The Nez Perce spoke a language called Nez Perce. They also knew the **sign language** that many Native American groups knew. A sign language uses hand movements instead of words.

Examples of Native American sign language

culture
the traditions, language, dress, ceremonies, and other ways of life that a group of people share

For the Nez Perce, storytelling was one way of passing down their **culture** to their children. During the long winter months, the older people passed the time by telling stories. They told the children stories about the mountains and rivers of their land. They also told them about the world of animals and **spirits**. The children learned about their culture by listening to the stories.

Arts and Crafts

The Nez Perce made many kinds of baskets. They made some out of bear grass, a plant with tough, dry leaves. Sometimes they dyed the bear grass to make red, yellow, and blue baskets. They also made baskets from the young branches of willow bushes. These baskets were used for storing and carrying things.

The Nez Perce wove patterns into their baskets.

The Nez Perce decorated their clothes with shells, elk's teeth, porcupine quills, and beads. They used these to make bird, animal, and flower patterns on their clothing. The decorations were part of their culture.

A Nez Perce girl of today wears a beaded dress with elk's teeth decorating it.

Key Concept 3 **Early trade was a way of exchanging both goods and ideas.**

Trade

Several times a year, the Nez Perce went to a place called The Dalles. The Dalles is on the Columbia River. It was an important center for **trade**. Native American groups from all around went there to trade with other groups.

trade
the buying, selling, or exchange of products

The Nez Perce took many **goods** with them. They took dried fish, salmon oil, and bows made of sheep horn. These were all things that could be traded or sold. The Nez Perce traded these things for goods made on the coast, such as seashells, wood carvings, and baskets.

goods
products that can be bought, sold, or exchanged

Bison skins were important goods to the Nez Perce.

Trade Between Native Americans

The Nez Perce traveled to the Great Plains to hunt bison and to trade. The Nez Perce got bison skins from the people of the Great Plains. They also traded their goods for clothing and food.

In early times, the Nez Perce may have gotten their first horses from southern nations like the Shoshone. Horses changed the way the Nez Perce lived. After the Nez Perce got horses, it was easier for them to move about. They could hunt more easily.
They could also travel farther to trade.

A group of Nez Perce riding horses

Think About the Key Concepts

Think about what you read. Think about the pictures and charts. Use these to answer the questions. Share what you think with others.

1. How did the homeland of the Native Americans affect their life there?

2. Why was storytelling important?

3. What was special about the culture, or way of life, of this Native American group?

4. How did trade affect the Native American group discussed in this book?

Comparison Chart

A chart allows you to find specific facts quickly and easily.
You can learn new ideas without having to read many words. Charts use words and a box-like layout to present ideas.

There are different kinds of charts.
This chart of Nez Perce clothing is a comparison chart. It compares different types of clothing and what they were made of.

How to Read a Comparison Chart

1. **Read the title.**

   The title tells you the subject, or what the chart is about.

2. **Read the column headings.**

   Columns go from top to bottom. The heading at the top of each column tells you what kind of information is in the column.

3. **Read the row headings.**

   Rows go from side to side. The headings in the left column name items you will get information about as you read across each row.

4. **Connect the information as you read.**

   Read across each row to find information about a subject. Read down each column to compare information.

Nez Perce Clothing

Type of Clothing	Deerskin	Fur	Elk's Teeth	Porcupine Quills	Beads	Vegetable Dye
Shirts	✔		✔	✔	✔	
Dresses	✔		✔	✔	✔	✔
Breechcloths	✔					
Leggings	✔			✔	✔	
Robes	✔					
Moccasins	✔	✔				
Decorations		✔	✔	✔	✔	

What's in the Chart?

Read the chart by following the steps on page 18. Write a few sentences about Nez Perce clothing. Compare your sentences with what another student wrote.

GENRE STUDY

Biographical Sources

The purpose of **biographical sources** is to give information about people's lives.

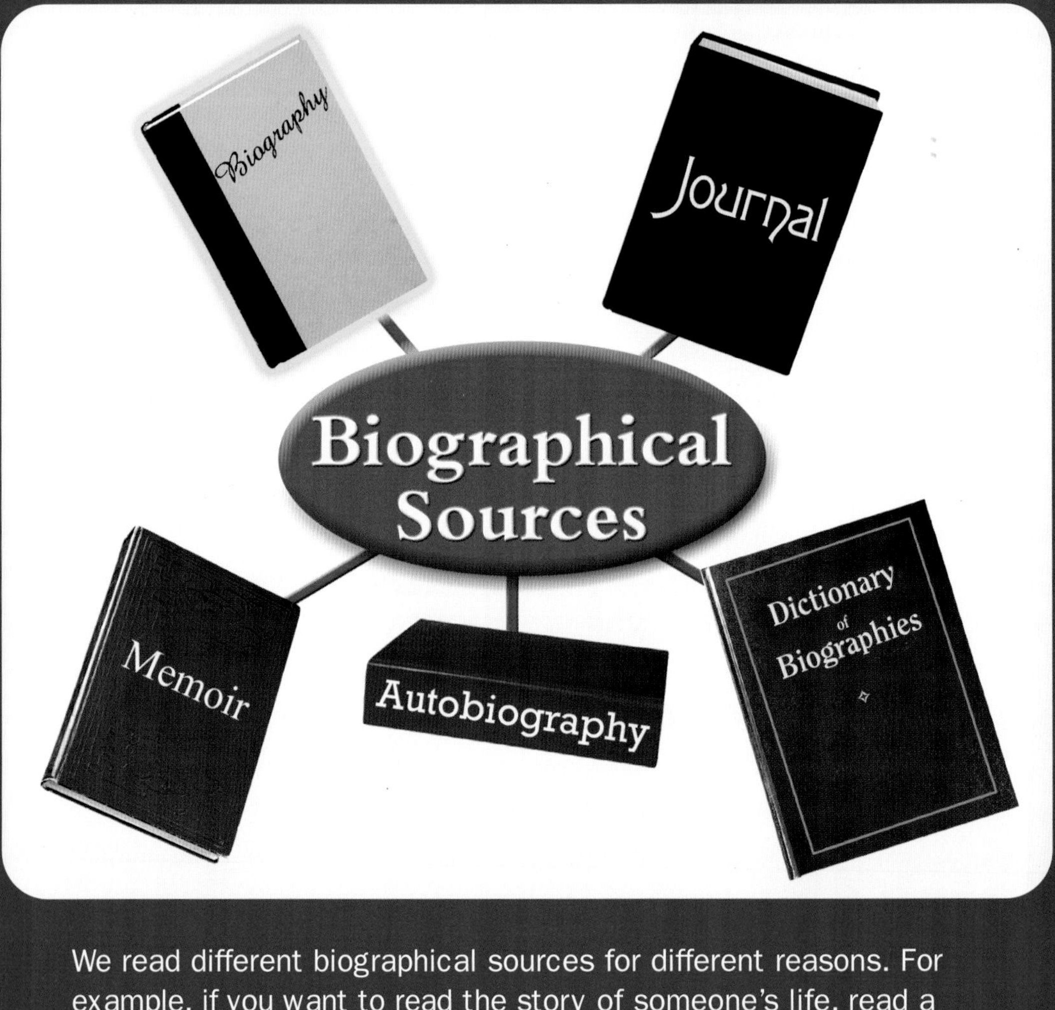

We read different biographical sources for different reasons. For example, if you want to read the story of someone's life, read a **biography**. But if you want to read one person's account of his or her own life, read that person's **autobiography**. Journals and memoirs are forms of autobiographies.

Nez Perce Biographies

A biography tells the story of a person's life. The story is often told in the order in which things happened. This order is called chronological order. The following biographies are of Nez Perce people.

Chief Joseph (1840–1904)

Name of the person

Dates tell of birth and death.

Chief Joseph

In the history of the Nez Perce people, one man's life story stands out. That man is Chief Joseph.

Chief Joseph is remembered as one of the great Nez Perce leaders. He was a man of peace, but when his people were in danger he took action. For much of his life he worked to help his people keep their homeland.

Chief Joseph was born in 1840. He was named Hin-mah-too-yah-lat-kekt. His name means "thunder rolling in the mountains."

Photographs and illustrations show the person at various times in his or her life.

Text has details about the person's life.

Most of the Nez Perce lived in Idaho. Chief Joseph was part of a smaller group that lived in the Wallowa Valley in Oregon. Joseph's father was a chief named Old Joseph. In 1855, Old Joseph signed a treaty, or agreement, with the United States government. The treaty said that the Wallowa Valley land belonged to the Nez Perce.

But at the beginning of the 1860s, gold was found in this area. The government wanted the land. They wanted to force the Nez Perce to settle down elsewhere. But Old Joseph would not move out.

In 1871, Old Joseph died and his son became chief. Chief Joseph had promised his father that he would not give up the land in the Wallowa Valley.

Chief Joseph had promised his father that he would not give up the land in the Wallowa Valley.

A **timeline** shows key events in the person's life.

Timeline

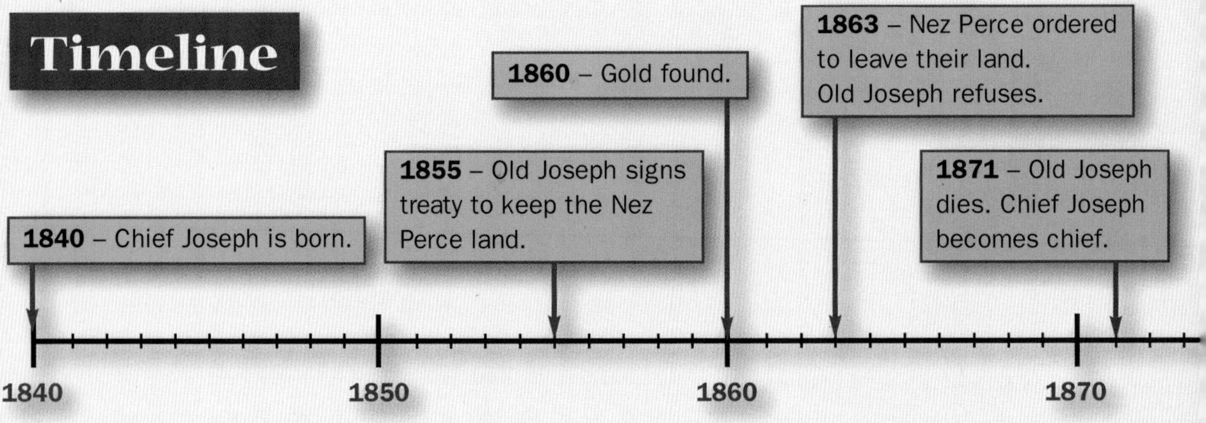

Chief Joseph wearing traditional Nez Perce clothing

In 1877, the United States government started to force the Nez Perce to move. Chief Joseph knew that the government had a strong army. He did not want the army to attack his people. So he agreed to move toward Idaho, where most Nez Perce lived. Though Joseph wanted peace, some warriors from his group attacked and killed some American settlers. Because of this attack, the army began to chase Chief Joseph's group.

Chief Joseph knew he needed to get his people out of the Wallowa Valley before they were killed. He decided to go north, to the country of Canada, where they would be safe.

The journey made by Chief Joseph and his people has become famous. About 700 men, women, and children traveled 1,700 miles (2,750 kilometers). They were chased by 2,000 United States soldiers. In three months, the Nez Perce fought four big battles. Chief Joseph finally surrendered on October 5, 1877.

Chief Joseph in 1903

But after Chief Joseph surrendered, the government would not allow his band of Nez Perce to go home. Instead, the government moved the group from place to place. Many people got sick and died. In 1879, Chief Joseph spoke to President Rutherford B. Hayes. He asked that his people be allowed to return to the Wallowa Valley.

In 1885, many people from Joseph's group, including Joseph himself, chose to go to northern Washington State. However, Oregon was still their homeland and they hoped that one day they would live there again.

The journey made by Chief Joseph and his people has become famous.

Chief Joseph never stopped hoping for the return of his people's homeland in Oregon. He died on September 21, 1904.

Jackson Sundown (1863–1923)

Jackson Sundown was born in 1863. He was a famous Nez Perce cowboy and horseman. From a young age, he was good with horses.

In 1877, Jackson Sundown fled with Chief Joseph, the leader of a group of Nez Perce. Chief Joseph's people were trying to get to Canada. Sundown's job on this trip was to take care of the horses. Not all the Nez Perce made it to Canada, but Sundown did.

Later, Sundown moved to the state of Montana. His fame as a horseman grew. He started entering rodeos. Rodeos are contests where cowboys attempt to ride wild bulls and horses. The wild horses are called broncos.

Soon, Sundown became a well-known rider. The crowds loved him. He looked good with his bright clothes and his hair tied in braids. Sundown was a good bronco rider. Each time he rode, he won. Soon, nobody wanted to ride against him.

Jackson Sundown

From a young age, Jackson Sundown was good with horses.

In 1915, Sundown was placed third in a competition. He decided to retire. But, in 1916, a friend talked him into entering one more competition. The friend was sure Sundown would win.

Sundown rode a horse named Angel at the competition. At the start of the ride, Angel's blindfold was taken off. The horse started to whirl and leap as it tried to throw Sundown off. But Sundown held on.

The crowd rose to their feet, chanting his name. They shouted, "Ride 'im, Sundown!" Sundown managed to stay on Angel until the end of the ride. He became the first Native American world-champion bronco rider.

Jackson Sundown riding in a rodeo in 1915

Apply the Key Concepts

Key Concept 1 The homelands of native people have influenced their food, clothing, and shelter.

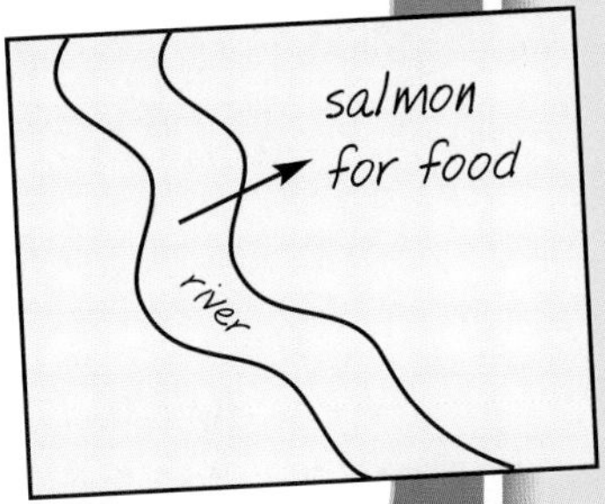

Activity

Choose three items the Nez Perce found or hunted in their homeland. Make a sketch of each of these items using this book and other sources as references. Then use arrows and labels to tell how the Nez Perce used these items in their daily lives.

Key Concept 2 The stories and arts of native people were an expression of culture and a way of passing on values.

Activity

Culture is how a group of people carries out its traditions and way of life. Use four examples of Nez Perce culture to create a Nez Perce Cultural Handbook. First write a sentence or two for each topic. Then use images and descriptions from *The Nez Perce* as guides for illustrating each topic. Make a cover for your handbook and remember to include the author's name!

Key Concept 3 Early trade was a way of exchanging both goods and ideas.

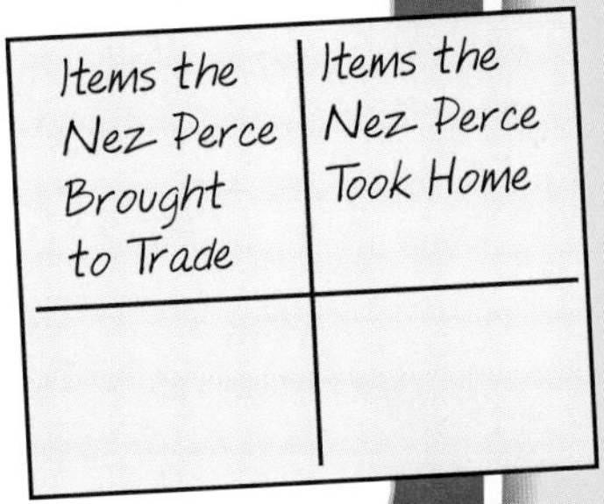

Activity

Create a two-column chart listing the goods the Nez Perce traded with other groups. Label the two columns: "Items the Nez Perce Brought to Trade" and "Items the Nez Perce Took Home." Include at least three items in each column.

RESEARCH AND WRITE

Write Your Autobiography

Many people like to write autobiographies, or stories of their own lives. You can write a short autobiography that focuses on three or four important events in your life. You will probably have to do some research, though. Family members and friends can help you remember details.

1. Study the Model

Look back at pages 21–26. What are the things you need to think about when writing a biography or autobiography? You will need to remember these as you write your autobiography. Now, read one of the biographies again. As you read it, make a note of the most important events that are mentioned. Look at the timeline. Make a note of the important events on the timeline.

Writing an Autobiography

- Choose some important events in your life.
- Write about the events in the order that they happened.
- Use a timeline to chart important dates.
- Use pictures with captions to illustrate your autobiography.

2. Research Your Topic

You already know some important events in your own life. But there will be details about the events that you won't remember. You will need to ask your parents, grandparents, neighbors, and friends.

Make a list of the events that you want to include in your autobiography. Then make a list of questions to ask others. Take notes on what you learn. Try to get as many dates as possible so that you can create a timeline. You may also have some photographs that you can use to illustrate your autobiography.

Events in My Life

1. Got a new little sister
2. Rode my first bike
3. Was in the class play

3. Write a Draft

Look over all the information you have. Now look back at one of the biographies again. Use it to help you write about yourself. Then tell about your important events in order. If you wish, tell about how events made you feel or what you learned from them. Be sure to use pronouns like *I* and *me*. At the end, tie the events together in a concluding paragraph. Then draw up a timeline. Write a few words about the most important events along with the dates they occurred.

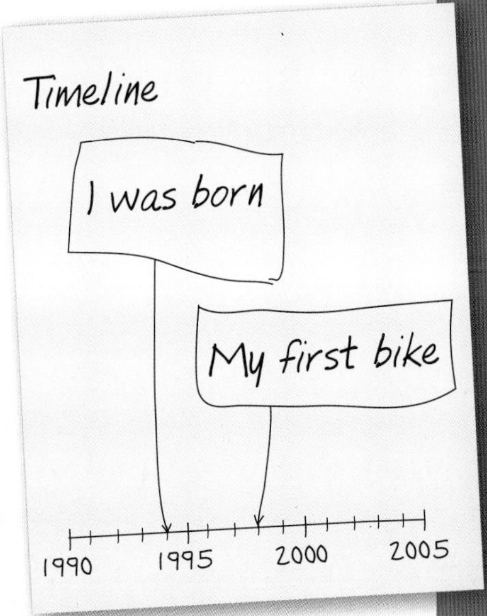

4. Revise and Edit

Read over your draft. What do you like? What would you like to change? Make these changes. Then read your draft again. This time, fix any mistakes. Look for words that are misspelled. Be sure each sentence starts with a capital letter. Be sure that you have your information in order.

SHARING YOUR WORK

Publish Your Autobiography

Before you can share your autobiography, you need to publish it.

Take time to think about what your finished autobiography will look like. Do you have photographs? Where will they go? Can you keep these photographs or should you copy or scan them? Where will you put the timeline? What will you call your work? When you have made these decisions, write the final copy of your autobiography. Then you will be ready to share.

1. **Give your autobiography a title.** The title should include your name because your autobiography is your story. The title should also relate to the events you have written about.

2. **Include photographs or drawings.** Use photographs of yourself and your family, or illustrate your autobiography with your own drawings.

3. **Add captions to pictures.** Remember, captions and labels tell what pictures are about.

4. **Organize the events on a timeline.** Write a short description of the most important events next to their dates on your timeline.

Share Your Autobiography

Now you are ready to share your autobiography. Get together with a group of your classmates. Read each other's autobiographies. When you have all finished reading, discuss the things that are the same in your lives and the things that are different.

Glossary

bison – a type of wild ox with long, shaggy hair and short horns

breechcloth – a piece of cloth worn around the hips like a short skirt

culture – the traditions, language, dress, ceremonies, and other ways of life that a group of people share

goods – products that can be bought, sold, or exchanged

homeland – the place a people or nation chooses to make its home

longhouses – long Native American houses built for a large group to live in

moccasins – soft leather shoes with soft soles

sign language – a language that uses hands and fingers to make shapes that mean different things

spirits – beings that are believed to exist in another world

tepees – cone-shaped tents made with animal skins stretched over frames of wooden poles

trade – the buying, selling, or exchange of products

Index